40 Days of HEBREW Devotions

Eli Lizorkin-Eyzenberg
and Pinchas Shir with Jaime Purcell

ISBN: 9798649330992

40 Days of Hebrew Devotions, Copyright © 2020 by Eliyahu Lizorkin-Eyzenberg. Cover design by Pinchas Shir. This book contains material protected under International and Federal Copyright Laws and Treaties. Any unauthorized reprint or use of this material is prohibited. No part of this book may be reproduced or transmitted in any form or by any means, electronic or mechanical, including photocopying, recording, or by any information storage and retrieval system without written permission from the author (dr.eli.israel@gmail.com).

Table of Contents

INTRODUCTION 5

DAY 1 – SLOW TO ANGER 7

DAY 2 – BLESSING & CURSE 9

DAY 3 – EL SHADDAI 11

DAY 4 – OFFERING 13

DAY 5 – IMAGE 16

DAY 6 – MERCY 19

DAY 7 – HOLY GARMENTS 22

DAY 8 – A SOLDIER 24

DAY 9 – SIN 26

DAY 10 – SATAN 28

DAY 11 – RIGHTEOUSNESS 30

DAY 12 – YOUNG AND GREAT 32

DAY 13 – RABBI 34

DAY 14 – LOVE 36

DAY 15 – THE GOSPEL 38

DAY 16 – TOGETHER 40

DAY 17 – JACOB & ISRAEL 42

DAY 18 – YESHUA 44

DAY 19 – ARMIES 46

DAY 20 – NATIONS	48
DAY 21 – ARMAGEDDON	50
DAY 22 – TORAH	52
DAY 23 – RAINBOW	54
DAY 24 – HOLY	56
DAY 25 – JUDAH	58
DAY 26 – HEBREW	60
DAY 27 – HALLELUIAH	62
DAY 28 – PENTECOST	64
DAY 29 – NISSI	66
DAY 30 – SHALOM	68
DAY 31 – ZION	70
DAY 32 – YIREH	72
DAY 33 – OBSERVANCE	74
DAY 35 – GLOW	78
DAY 36 – HAKIPPURIM	80
DAY 37 – IDF	82
DAY 38 – KNESSET	84
DAY 39 - GEMATRIA	86
DAY 40 - CHANUKAH	88

Introduction

This short devotional is a little different from others you may have encountered. It focuses not on some great theological truths or even practical life matters but looks at select Hebrew words used in the Bible. It shows you something you may not have seen before by exploring the meanings of Hebrew words hidden behind the familiar English text.

Our brief commentaries and explanations are supplied with some short prayers. They may appear a bit unusual to you at first. They follow the Jewish tradition of praying communally as one people (even when praying alone). The famous "Lord's Prayer" uses only plural pronouns and follows this same practice. So feel free to use the prayers that we supplied or pray in your own words if you prefer. Just don't forget to reflect after reading each section.

We sincerely hope that you will hear God speak through the Hebrew words you encounter as they connect the dots and take you to new places. Thanks for letting us be your guides on this journey.

Pinchas Shir
Eli Lizorkin-Eyzenberg

DAY 1 – SLOW TO ANGER

SCRIPTURE: *Then the LORD passed by in front of him and proclaimed, "The LORD, the LORD God, compassionate and gracious, slow to anger, and abounding in lovingkindness and truth; who keeps lovingkindness for thousands, who forgives iniquity, transgression and sin; yet He will by no means leave the guilty unpunished, visiting the iniquity of fathers on the children and on the grandchildren to the third and fourth generations." (Ex. 34:6-7)*

Over and over, throughout the Day of Atonement services, the worshiping community breaks out into a familiar song in Hebrew, reciting the very same words YHVH pronounced as He shielded Moses from the power of his own presence (Exodus 34:6-7). One of the truly intriguing things that God declared about himself is hidden beneath the English translation. God said that He was אֶרֶךְ אַפַּיִם (pronounced: *erech apaim*).

If you can't read Hebrew, don't feel bad (although God knows you owe it to yourself to start learning at least some Hebrew already!). Not many people know the meaning of this ancient Hebrew phrase. You see, *erech apaim* literally means, "[He] has a long nose." What in the world could that possibly mean in reference to God? The answer is actually very simple.

Imagine looking at someone getting angry. Their nose is visibly enlarged. The nostrils widen as their indignation is expressed in facial changes. The saying that God has a very long nose (note: in this passage nose is in plural form) is a beautiful ancient Hebrew idiomatic expression pointing out that God is very slow to anger.

I am so happy that most of our English translations get this idiom right: "The LORD, the LORD God, compassionate and gracious, slow to anger (אֶרֶךְ אַפַּיִם), and abounding in lovingkindness and truth; who keeps lovingkindness for thousands, who forgives iniquity, transgression, and sin." (Ex. 34:6-7)

PRAYER: *O, Lord of the Universe, Creator of all things, we praise you that you revealed your name to Moses your servant, and to us so long ago. Though we do not comprehend your name fully, it still tells us so much about you. As we come before you overwhelmed by your presence, just as Moses was so long ago may your very long nose be a reminder of your kindness. As seasons and time pass and we need your patience and longsuffering again and again. May we experience your immense mercy and grace when we need them most! And may our noses also get longer and longer as we get to know you in an even more intimate way. As we encounter our neighbors and friends may we learn how to be more gracious and slow to anger by following your example.*

DAY 2 – BLESSING & CURSE

SCRIPTURE: *Now the LORD said to Abram, "Go forth from your country, and from your relatives and from your father's house, to the land which I will show you; And I will make you a great nation, and I will bless you, and make your name great; And so you shall be a blessing; And I will bless those who bless you, and the one who curses you I will curse. And in you all the families of the earth will be blessed" (Genesis 12:1-3).*

Sometimes we take the idea of what is a blessing for granted. We even say "God bless you" when someone sneezes, but what is a blessing?

God promised to Abraham in Gen.12:3 "I will bless those who bless you (וַאֲבָרְכָה מְבָרְכֶיךָ), and the one who curses you I will curse (וּמְקַלֶּלְךָ אָאֹר). The Biblical command enjoined on all who worship God of Abraham is crystal clear – they must bless the descendants of Abraham, the people of Israel.

In Hebrew, the verb to bless is לברך (pronounced: *levarech*) comes from the root בָּרַךְ *(barach)*. This root is directly connected to the word "knee" בֶּרֶךְ *(berech)* which implies kneeling and rendering service to someone. God is not saying he is going to "bend his knee", but as we think about it, the meaning of this verse can be something like "I will serve those who serve you."

In this promise, the opposite of a blessing is a curse. God also tells Abraham that everyone who curses (מְקַלֶּלְךָ) him will be cursed (אָאֹר) by God in return. The strength of the promise, however, is somewhat lost in translation.

The first word for "curse" (מְקַלֶּלְךָ) comes from a root that literally means to "make light of someone or something heavy". But the second word for "curse" (אָאֹר) which God renders comes from a completely different root that can mean something like "to utterly destroy". Taking into consideration the translation can flow like this: "I will serve those who will serve you and the ones who make light of you I will utterly destroy."

Could the guarantee of God's protection over the children of Abraham be made any clearer?!

PRAYER: *Almighty LORD, Most High, the author of our faith, you wield power over all who live and hold us in your hand. The power to bless and to curse is in your hands, the power to increase or to diminish also. You chose to preserve the fortunes of some and allow plans of others to unravel and fall apart at the seams. Why we may never understand. The seed of Abraham has a special place in your plans for our world and you determine whom to bless and whom to curse depending on how they treat the patriarch's descendants.*

Thank you for your warning, for your promise, for making your will plain to us in this regard. Guard us, Oh, LORD that we may not bring curses to ourselves by going against you who reign on high in light and power, in grace and justice.

DAY 3 – EL SHADDAI

SCRIPTURE: *Now when Abram was ninety-nine years old, the LORD appeared to Abram and said to him, "I am God Almighty; Walk before Me, and be blameless. "I will establish My covenant between Me and you, and I will multiply you exceedingly." Abram fell on his face, and God talked with him, saying, "As for Me, behold, My covenant is with you, And you will be the father of a multitude of nations. "No longer shall your name be called Abram, but your name shall be Abraham; For I have made you the father of a multitude of nations (Genesis 17:1-5).*

El Shaddai (אֵל שַׁדַּי) is just one of the many names of God in Hebrew. Of course, אֵל *(el)* means "God". The rest, however, is slightly more complicated.

In our Bibles, אֵל שַׁדַּי *(El Shaddai)* is most often translated as "God Almighty". But that may not be the best translation after all. Translators who think that El Shaddai means God Almighty hold that Hebrew word שַׁדַּי *(shaddai)* is likely connected to the verb לִשְׁדוד *(lishdod),* which means "to destroy" or "overpower". For example, the Hebrew word for "bandit" has the same root –שׁודֵד *(shoded).* You can see that even though *El Shaddai* (אֵל שַׁדַּי) has only one "D" sound in Hebrew, in English it is spelled as if the D is doubled (Shaddai instead of Shadai). Yet this meaning does not seem to make sense. Why would God reveal himself to Abraham by such a name?

It is also possible that שַׁדַּי *(shaddai)* has another origin and a vastly different meaning. Hebrew word שַׁד *(shad)* means "breast", "chest", or "bosom". Moreover, whenever a word ends with "ai" in Hebrew it almost always reflects plural, often a pair and even personal possession - "my." Therefore, this mysterious name אֵל שַׁדַּי *(El Shaddai)* could literally mean "God (is) my 'Breast/s'".

Does that make more sense than God the Destroyer or God Almighty? It does. A breast is a symbol of life sustenance, maternal nurturing, and parental (motherly) love. Associating God with the source of such provision makes perfect sense and instead of "God Almighty", *El Shaddai* can be translated as "God All-sufficient". (This radically strange biblical language is present in other places too for example in the above-mentioned case when God reveals himself to Moses as patience and long-suffering God, which in Hebrew literally means that he (God) has a long nose). This description of God fits much better with the words of comfort God spoke to Abraham as he wondered in his heart how he will venture out on his own and go to a distant land without the support of his family.

PRAYER: *All-sufficient God, you hold the power to smite and to heal, to afflict, and to nourish in your hands. LORD, you provide all things that we have in our lives. You sustain us, though we may not always recognize or acknowledge your provision. Master draw us closer to yourself; help us understand your goodness. May your great name be praised and never depart from our lips. May those around us praise you because of how we give honor to you, our God.*

DAY 4 – OFFERING

SCRIPTURE: *He was also saying to them, "You are experts at setting aside the commandment of God in order to keep your tradition. For Moses said, 'HONOR YOUR FATHER AND YOUR MOTHER'; and, 'HE WHO SPEAKS EVIL OF FATHER OR MOTHER, IS TO BE PUT TO DEATH'; but you say, 'If a man says to his father or his mother, whatever I have that would help you is Corban (that is to say, given to God),' you no longer permit him to do anything for his father or his mother; thus invalidating the word of God by your tradition which you have handed down; and you do many things such as that" (Mark 7:9-13).*

The Hebrew word often translated "offering" is קָרְבָּן (pronounced: *korban*). It is a fascinating word, full of rich meaning. There are many words in Hebrew with this root קרב *(karav)*. For example, the verb "to offer" or "to sacrifice" is להקריב (pronounced: *lehakriv*), while the verb to "draw near" or to "come close" is להתקרב (pronounced: *lehitkarev*). One can imagine that an "offering" is a symbolic way of "coming closer".

When a family connection is described in Hebrew, we use the phrase – קרוב-משפחה *(krov mishpaha)*, which literally means "close family". Considering the Hebrew meaning, an "offering" קָרְבָּן *(korban)* should be thought of as something people use to get near towards God.

Most Eastern cultures still preserve an interesting ancient idea that one cannot go to someone else's house for fellowship empty-handed. One must have something to offer in their hand in order to enter into the house of a neighbor or relative. In the same Eastern tradition preserves something else that is very beautiful. Not only the guest cannot come empty-handed, but the host cannot allow him or her to leave empty-handed either! The enterprise of fellowship turns out to be a wonderful exchange of, usually culinary, gifts.

PRAYER: *Call out to us, Mighty God, and we will come, draw us near to yourself, Oh, LORD, and we will approach! How beautiful are your courts, Oh, LORD, your gates, your dwelling places. We desire closeness to you, LORD when we come with sacrifices of our praise and thanksgiving. LORD, God of Israel, we offer our lives as living sacrifices on your altar of mercy and pray that our gifts find favor in your eyes.*

When we draw close to you, Oh, King, draw close to us and welcome us into your sweet presence. We come with gifts. May we find favor in your eyes so that we too will not depart empty-handed.

MY REQUEST

Dear reader, may I ask you for a favor? Would you take three minutes of your time and provide an encouraging feedback to other people shopping on Amazon.com about this book (assuming you like it of course!)?

Here is how: 1. Go to **Amazon.com** and search for the title of this book – **"40 Days of Hebrew Devotions"**. 2. Click on the title, click on the "ratings" link (right under the author's name) and click **"Write a customer review"** button. 3. Rate the book and leave a few words.

This will really help me a lot, especially if you genuinely love this book! After writing a review please drop me a personal note and let me know - **dr.eli.israel@gmail.com**. I would appreciate your help with this.

Dr. Eli Lizorkin-Eyzenberg

DAY 5 – IMAGE

SCRIPTURE: *Then God said, "Let Us make man in Our image, according to Our likeness; and let them rule over the fish of the sea and over the birds of the sky and over the cattle and over all the earth, and over every creeping thing that creeps on the earth." God created man in His own image, in the image of God He created him; male and female He created them. God blessed them; and God said to them, "Be fruitful and multiply, and fill the earth, and subdue it; and rule over the fish of the sea and over the birds of the sky and over every living thing that moves on the earth" (Genesis 1:26-28).*

At the very beginning of the Bible, we are told that human beings are an honored part of God's creation. In fact, we are told that God created people in his own image צֶלֶם אֱלֹהִים *(tzelem Elohim)*. The Hebrew word for "image" צלם (pronounced: *tzelem*) is connected with another Hebrew word - צל (pronounced: *tzel*), meaning "shadow".

Do you see any connection? When light falls upon an object, a shadow appears next to it. According to the Bible, a human being is nothing less than the image/figure of God because in many ways he/she wondrously reflects/shadows God's perfection and beauty.

Another biblical term where we can see this same connection is name Bezalel, a craftsman appointed by God to create the Tabernacle and all its furnishings (Ex. 31). Literally, בזלל (pronounced: *Betzalel*) means "in the shadow of God". The Tabernacle and everything inside it allowed the ancient Israelites to approach God and have a tangible connection with their Maker.

When humans worship the God of Heaven and Earth they step into the very shadow of God, they stand in proximity, in his presence. The amazing part, we were all made to be that way from the very beginning.

PRAYER: *Prince of Peace, Oh, to find our rest in the shadows of your wings! LORD, we look to you for many things in life: for provision when we have a need, for healing when we are hurting, for justice when we are mistreated. We come before you in prayer with so many requests. But how rarely do we simply find peace and satisfaction in your shadow, in your still presence? Father of Light, you have been a protector to us from the beginning. How many times have you spread your wings over us when we were in danger? How many times have you shielded us from the attacks of the enemy?*

Being in your shadow tells us that you are near. Are we worthy to see you as you are, Master of Legions? Perhaps we will be overwhelmed if we see your full glory and your shadow is enough for us. In your shadow is where we find our safety. Oh, LORD, do not allow us to depart from your presence. Let us stay close at all times. Praise be to you whose hand is never too short to save and redeem your creation.

MY REQUEST

Dear reader, may I ask you for a favor? Would you take three minutes of your time and provide an encouraging feedback to other people shopping on Amazon.com about this book (assuming you like it of course!)?

Here is how: 1. Go to **Amazon.com** and search for the title of this book – **"40 Days of Hebrew Devotions"**. 2. Click on the title, click on the "ratings" link (right under the author's name) and click **"Write a customer review"** button. 3. Rate the book and leave a few words.

This will really help me a lot, especially if you genuinely love this book! After writing a review please drop me a personal note and let me know - **dr.eli.israel@gmail.com**. I would appreciate your help with this.

Dr. Eli Lizorkin-Eyzenberg

DAY 6 – MERCY

SCRIPTURE: *The LORD descended in the cloud and stood there with him as he called upon the name of the LORD. Then the LORD passed by in front of him and proclaimed, "The LORD, the LORD God, compassionate and gracious, slow to anger, and abounding in lovingkindness and truth; who keeps lovingkindness for thousands, who forgives iniquity, transgression and sin; yet He will by no means leave the guilty unpunished, visiting the iniquity of fathers on the children and on the grandchildren to the third and fourth generations" (Ex. 34:5-7).*

Moses spent many days in God's presence, receiving instructions from him. But this time God's appearance was special. God revealed himself to Moses like never before. What happened can be best described that Moses saw God from the back with peripheral vision.

He heard the LORD's proclamation which established Israel's God as a the Merciful One (אֵל רַחוּם; *El rachum*). Hebrew word רַחֲמִים (pronounced: *rachamim*) means "mercy" or "compassion" and the verb לרחם (pronounced: *lerachem*) means to "have mercy" or sometimes "pity". In Hebrew רחים (pronounced: *rachim*) means something like "darling" or "beloved".

What is most intriguing is that the root that conveys mercy רַחֲמִים *(rachamim)* also connects to the idea of pregnancy. In Hebrew, a mother's womb is called רֶחֶם (pronounced: *rechem*). There too, the miracle of conception and protection of the child is defined in terms of mercy and compassion.

PRAYER: *Av Harachamim, Father of Compassion, we look to you with hope and joy as children do to parents. Look upon us with delight and find pleasure in our trust, our reliance, and our dependence. For we are weak and feeble as young babes, as if emerging from the womb, we require much care. You are as a mother to us all, you nurture and sustain us. You feed us and clothe us. You train us and teach us so much. In all we do we hope to make you proud as a parent. We seek your approval and praise.*

But as all minors do, we have no shortage of our troubles; as adolescents, we rebel, we test the wisdom of your ways and sometimes stray from the paths you have laid before us. That is why Oh, LORD, we ask that your wisdom and mercy may follow us all the days of our lives as we learn to walk in faith with you. We truly seek to glorify you as your children and ask that you protect us in your mercy as a mother protects her child in her womb. Who is like you, LORD? We are continually struck by your strength and justice, by your mercy and compassion, by your love for the humble and your sternness to the arrogant.

MY REQUEST

Dear reader, may I ask you for a favor? Would you take three minutes of your time and provide an encouraging feedback to other people shopping on Amazon.com about this book (assuming you like it of course!)?

Here is how: 1. Go to **Amazon.com** and search for the title of this book – **"40 Days of Hebrew Devotions"**. 2. Click on the title, click on the "ratings" link (right under the author's name) and click **"Write a customer review"** button. 3. Rate the book and leave a few words.

This will really help me a lot, especially if you genuinely love this book! After writing a review please drop me a personal note and let me know - **dr.eli.israel@gmail.com**. I would appreciate your help with this.

Dr. Eli Lizorkin-Eyzenberg

DAY 7 – HOLY GARMENTS

SCRIPTURE: *These are the garments which they shall make: a breast piece and an ephod and a robe and a tunic of checkered work, a turban and a sash, and they shall make holy garments for Aaron your brother and his sons, that he may minister as priest to Me (Exodus 28:4).*

Many religions have special garments. In Israel, the priests wore elaborate robes to signify their proximity to God too. But then even common Israelites were commanded to wear some very distinctive clothing, because the entire nation was designated by God in some sense as priestly. A good example of such is a commandment about "tzitzit" (צִיצִית) – a tassel which hangs from the corners of four-cornered garments (Num. 15:38). You may have also noticed that religious Jewish men often cover their heads with a small hat called "kippah" (כיפה) in Hebrew. Unlike tzitzit, a kippah is not expressly commanded in the Hebrew Bible.

In ancient times, covering one's head was mandatory only for the priests (Exodus 28:4, 37, 40). But with the disappearance of Temple, another custom emerged. The covering the head symbolically projected priestly duties on every male Jew. Sometimes this traditional head-covering is called "yarmulke" (ירמולכא). What does "yarmulke" mean in Hebrew? The answer is nothing. The best we know the word comes from the Judeo-German language called Yiddish which in turn built it from two Aramaic words – "fear" *(yir)* and "the king" *(malkah)*. Ending "ah" in "malkah" is an Aramaic equivalent to "the" in English and "ha" in Hebrew, being a definite article.) Thus a kippah or a yarmulke is a cultural and religious garment, worn by those who wish to express visually that they "fear the King"

Just as holy garments of Aaron and other distinctive clothing commanded to Israelites this hat or skullcap made of cloth serves a singular purpose, to distinguish between people and their Creator, to proclaim who is the King and who is not.

PRAYER: *Why do we seek you, Oh, LORD? Perhaps because we know - we have a Maker! And when we find you, we wish to hide ourselves and not be seen by you. We are but mere dust, clay from the earth, some matter shaped into a form, with moisture, breath of life and hearts that beat within our chests. You, on the other hand, are the Wisdom of the Ages, the Presence of the Power that speck of dust cannot begin to comprehend. In the garden, you have given our ancestors a covering to hide their guilt and insignificance before you. Since those days we wear garments. You decreed that your priests should come into your abode with covered heads to show the reverence and to acknowledge their fear.*

We fear you today, Almighty, shaking as leaves upon a tree before the LORD of light. You have all power over us, no doubt. The coverings, whether made by you, or by us, display the awe we have of your holiness and glory, so see them as we do. We cannot hide from Maker of our lives any more than we can rid ourselves from the very breath that stirs within us. Your spirit is within, we have a spark of you in the recesses of our being, yet were are not the same. We know you are our King and we are servants of the Mighty God.

DAY 8 – A SOLDIER

SCRIPTURE: *An excellent wife, who can find? For her worth is far above jewels. The heart of her husband trusts in her, and he will have no lack of gain. She does him good and not evil all the days of her life. She looks for wool and flax and works with her hands in delight. She is like merchant ships; She brings her food from afar (Proverbs 31:10-14).*

A famous biblical passage, Proverbs 31 describes an amazing wife. Many women who read this passage wonder how they can measure up to this extraordinary lady. This woman is the concept of God's wisdom personified. In Hebrew this extraordinary woman is called "eshet chayil" (אשת חיל) – the "woman of virtue" or "excellent wife", depending on the translation. It is indeed a very interesting designation.

In Biblical Hebrew, the root חיל "chayal" is associated with a variety of words such as pain, birth-pangs, fortification, bulwark, an outer wall of defense, honesty, and even wealth. In modern Hebrew, a male soldier is called "chayal" (חיל) and a female soldier is "chayelet" (חילת). Since Hebrew is a root language, we can clearly see how this word is connected with other related meanings.

For example, חיול "chiul" is "mobilization, and "chayil avir" (חיל אביר) is air force (lit. the army of the air), "chayil hayam" (חיל הים) is navy (lit. the army of the sea), "chayil raglim" (חיל רגלים) – infantry (lit. the army on foot).

Taking all this into consideration, the Proverbs 31 woman is something like a soldier, a woman-army, woman-fortress, woman-wealth, and security. In some sense, we all are called to be soldiers of God's light, daily reflecting his great wisdom in all our steps and our dealings. Whether men or women of God, let us think of ourselves as forces under the Almighty's command. We can share in his mighty victory. In a world which only knows darkness all over the land, at sea, and even in the air we can be mobilized and ready to defend or follow our Lord into battle if needed.

PRAYER: *Redeemer, King, and Mighty Fortress are you God. The righteous may find shelter, safety, and protection within your walls. The weak look to you for support and even the strong turn to you for guidance. You are the Prince of Peace and a Mighty Warrior all at once. Who is like you? LORD, we are continually struck by your strength and justice, by your mercy and compassion, by your love for the humble and sternness to the arrogant.*

May we grow to know you in all your glory as we live our lives, as we move through the winding trails of life you placed us on and even treacherous waters we must cross. Thank you for being our strength when we have none. Thank you for being our worth when we feel that there is nothing redeemable in us. Thank you for being the example of virtue and goodness to us, a powerful example we seek to resemble in the depths of our souls. Blessed be your name, LORD.

DAY 9 – SIN

SCRIPTURE: *Behold, I was brought forth in iniquity, and in sin my mother conceived me. Behold, You desire truth in the innermost being, and in the hidden part You will make me know wisdom. Purify me with hyssop, and I shall be clean; Wash me, and I shall be whiter than snow. Make me to hear joy and gladness, Let the bones which You have broken rejoice. Hide Your face from my sins and blot out all my iniquities (Psalm 51:5-9).*

If you ask people to define the concept of sin, most will start going through a list of negative commandments citing evil deeds such as murder, theft, and others. But is that what "sin" really means?

The Hebrew language shows us something more as we look at the meaning of "sin" חֵטְא (pronounced: *chet*). In Hebrew, a related word לְהַחֲטִיא *(lehachita)* means making a mistake as if by missing the target.

For example, Judges 20:16 ascribes this quality to warriors from the tribe of Benjamin, "Out of all these people 700 choice men were left-handed; each one could sling a stone at a hair and not miss." A phrase in this verse - לֹא יַחֲטִא (pronounced: *lo yachti*) means "not missing the target". Related to "sin" חֵטְא *(chet)* is the longer form- חַטָּאת (pronounced: *chatat*). Torah uses this word for "sin offering" (Lev 4:3). In Leviticus 14:49 Israelites are instructed how to cleanse a house from strange mold, "To cleanse the house then, he shall take two birds…" The phrase "to cleanse the house" is לְחַטֵּא אֶת־הַבַּיִת *(lechateh et habait)* in Hebrew has this word חֵטְא

(chet) which we usually translate as "sin" or "sin offering".

In English "sin" is in no way connected to "cleansing" of any kind but in modern Hebrew, the word for "disinfection" is חִטֵּא (pronounced: *chiteh*). It is incredible to see how the Hebrew language can work with word roots. The same word that ordinarily means "sin", "making an error", and "missing the mark" is connected to the word for "sin offering" in the Temple and can even communicate "purification".

PRAYER: *Create pure heart within us, Oh, God. We make mistakes too often, we wander off, we get hurt and hurt others. At times we become completely disoriented and lost. But as a good shepherd, you go after us, you find us LORD and carry us home. Yes, we miss the mark, even when we purposefully aim to please.*

Your words, Oh, God are as the knife that cuts, convicts, and prunes our hearts. At other times they are like ointment and a healing balm we need. Thank you, LORD, that you seek to purify us, helping us draw closer to you even though we miss the mark so often. Give us the fervor, Oh, Shepherd of Israel, to listen for your voice and the timeless teaching you gave us, and to obey your voice as those who know their Master.

DAY 10 – SATAN

SCRIPTURE: *Now there was a day when the sons of God came to present themselves before the LORD, and Satan also came among them. The LORD said to Satan, "From where do you come?" Then Satan answered the LORD and said, "From roaming about on the earth and walking around on it." The LORD said to Satan, "Have you considered My servant Job? For there is no one like him on the earth, a blameless and upright man, fearing God and turning away from evil." (Job 1:6-8)*

Many people have the impression that Satan is a name, just like Job. But that is not the case. The word שָׂטָן (pronounced: *sahtan*) means "adversary" and relates to verb לְשָׂטָן (*lesahtan*) which means "to oppose".

We see this meaning clearly in the passage where Balaam the seer was contracted for his services to curse Israel's armies by the rulers of Moab and Midian (Numbers 22). When it became clear that Balaam, and not the donkey was blind and stubborn, the Angel of the LORD said to Balaam: "I have come here to oppose you (לְשָׂטָן; *lesahtan*) because your path is a reckless one before me."

The verb "to oppose" makes sense but sometimes in the Hebrew Bible, Satan is treated as a name by adding the prefix "the" (ה), making it "the Satan" as in Job 1:6 when we are told that וַיָּבוֹא גַם־הַשָּׂטָן בְּתוֹכָם *(vayavo gam-hasahtan betocham)* "Satan also came among them".

Let us not resemble Balaam and be easily led astray. Let us know that with keeping our eyes on God, we can overcome all attempts of any adversary who would seek to sway us from the LORD's path.

PRAYER: *The first and the last are you, LORD, and who can claim to compare with your greatness? If our God is for us, then who can be against us? Though the adversary can come against us as a thief in the night, as a flood, as a destructive tempest with the fury of the wind, we can withstand it. Your hand and your staff protect us, your radiance overwhelms the fear that may otherwise be paralyzing. You have made promises, Oh God, amazing promises to your children, assurances of protection and preservation of our souls.*

Speak peace to us, Oh, Maker, and have mercy. Though some may come against us in this life, seeking to destroy, to demolish, to crush our efforts of serving you faithfully they will not succeed. We have you, Oh, Redeemer, to thank for that. Give us your wisdom, LORD to recognize our foes and teach us how to deal with them with the strength and wisdom that you provide, and may you be glorified in our victories.

DAY 11 – RIGHTEOUSNESS

SCRIPTURE: *After these things the word of the LORD came to Abram in a vision, saying, "Do not fear, Abram, I am a shield to you; Your reward shall be very great." Abram said, "O Lord GOD, what will You give me, since I am childless, and the heir of my house is Eliezer of Damascus?" And Abram said, "Since You have given no offspring to me, one born in my house is my heir." Then behold, the word of the LORD came to him, saying, "This man will not be your heir; but one who will come forth from your own body, he shall be your heir." And He took him outside and said, "Now look toward the heavens, and count the stars, if you are able to count them." And He said to him, "So shall your descendants be." Then he believed in the LORD; and He reckoned it to him as righteousness (Genesis 15:1-6).*

In the common line of thinking, the English word "righteousness" is equated with "holiness" which is often understood as perfection and life without sin. In fact, for most people, the opposite of the "sinner" is a "righteous person".

But as we read the Bible there is a peculiar aspect of "righteousness" that the Hebrew language reveals. Gen 15:6 says, "Then he (Abraham) believed in the LORD, and He reckoned it to him as righteousness." What exactly happened?

In Hebrew, "righteousness" is צְדָקָה (pronounced: *tzedakah*) and a righteous person is called a צַדִּיק *(tzadik)*. The Hebrew root צדק *(tzadak)* can also be understood as "justice", "fairness", and "equity". Another related word צֶדֶק (pronounced: *tzedek*), for example, means "right", "piety", "straight and proper action". The actions of the upright, or deeds which are just, are called צְדָקוֹת (pronounced: *tzedakot*) in Hebrew.

Hebrew does not have a separate word for benevolent giving, the word "righteousness" צְדָקָה (pronounced: *tzedakah*) is used to describe such acts of kindness as well. When one practices charitable giving to those who do not have enough, one promotes the atmosphere of fairness, rightness, and equity in the world.

Therefore, when we or anyone else stands "justified" before God it is not because we've been made or even declared sinless, but because were deemed "right", "fair" or "righteous".

PRAYER: *Rock of Ages on whom we can stand, you are a righteous judge who hears our appeals. LORD, you are our loving father. You have taught us the truth, the principles of the good life, but your words require reason and sound judgment to make them flourish. We desperately wish to be like you, but being just and fair, being steadfast and not swayed by anger or pain is not something that comes easily to us. We are but clay and dirt, a poor imitation of your grandeur.*

We know that long ago you deemed Abraham's faith as righteousness and we hope that we can be like him in steadfast obedience and living. Show us to trust you as he did by following you willingly to the ends of the earth, not knowing what tomorrow holds. May we grow old in steady trust and righteousness you grant us.

DAY 12 – YOUNG AND GREAT

SCRIPTURE: *And Isaac prayed to the LORD for his wife, because she was barren. And the LORD granted his prayer, and Rebekah his wife conceived. The children struggled together within her, and she said, "If it is thus, why is this happening to me?" So she went to inquire of the LORD. And the LORD said to her, "Two nations are in your womb, and two peoples from within you shall be divided; the one shall be stronger than the other, the older shall serve the younger." (Genesis 25: 21-23)*

Translations obscure the fact that some of the original wording in Hebrew presents challenges and cannot always be translated with certainty. Most people are unaware that even faithful translators (and most of them truly are) must make difficult decisions, choosing from several options which the original text allows.

Gen. 25:23 is one example of the kind of challenge that translators often face. Putting things literally, we read: "Two peoples are in your stomach" (שְׁנֵי גֹיִים בְּבִטְנֵךְ). "two peoples will be separated from you" (וּשְׁנֵי לְאֻמִּים מִמֵּעַיִךְ יִפָּרֵדוּ) "one people over another will exercise strength" (וּלְאֹם מִלְאֹם יֶאֱמָץ). The last part of this verse introduces a considerable ambiguity. Most translations render it as "the older will serve the younger." (וְרַב יַעֲבֹד צָעִיר).

The problem is that definite articles are absent in these phrases in Hebrew, as well as the direct object marker את *(et)* which is needed there grammatically before the word "younger" (צָעִיר) for it to make any sense. Without the marker את *(et)* the sentence lacks clarity. In such a poetic voice, it can mean that "younger will serve the older" the other way around because the object is not clear!

Another confusing fact is that the opposite of "young" צָעִיר *(tzair)* is usually "old," but the Hebrew original has "great" רַב *(rav)*. "Greatness" is not the same thing as "seniority". In other words, because of grammatical ambiguity, the translation can work both ways. It can be "the older will serve the younger" or "the younger will serve the older"!

The choice translator must make by choosing just one version of what the texts can mean unintentionally hides something that probably was meant to challenge the reader/hearer of this Torah story.

PRAYER: *Great are your works, Oh, LORD. Though we may not always grasp your greatness, you are wondrous. Revealer of truth and Author of Wisdom, we look to you to know the mysteries of the universe. Oh, Creator, we are inquisitive people, curious, and ambitious in our endeavors to understand this world and even the one beyond.*

Alas, our minds are limited in grasping your deep truths. For our world is the world of shadows, one in which we see the truth through the glass and darkly. Only occasionally we see the light that is really there. How can we pretend to know the future? And especially your mind and your purposes, unless you choose to make it known to us? Help us see the truth plainly and grant us clarity, Oh, LORD.

DAY 13 – RABBI

SCRIPTURE: *Now there was a man of the Pharisees, named Nicodemus, a ruler of the Jews; this man came to Jesus by night and said to Him, "Rabbi, we know that You have come from God as a teacher; for no one can do these signs that You do unless God is with him." Jesus answered and said to him, "Truly, truly, I say to you, unless one is born again he cannot see the kingdom of God" (John 3:1-3).*

The term רַבִּי *(rabbi)* "my teacher" is ancient. Its original meaning translated from Hebrew literally means "one of abundance". In other words, רַבִּי *(rabbi)* in the ancient world was not some religious dignitary, but a "person of overabounding substance" - someone who has much to offer.

In Hebrew, oftentimes רַב *(rav)* is a measure relating to numerical quantity or length. For example, in the Torah, the cloud of God's presence stood over the tabernacle for יָמִים רַבִּים *(yamim rabim)* "many days" (Num 19:19).

At other times word רַב *(rav)* signifies authority, such as its use in ancient Hebrew when רַב בַּיִת *(rav bayt)* was used for the "head servant" and רַב הַחֹבֵל *(rav hachovel)* for the "captain of a ship". King Nebuchadnezzar promoted Daniel, making him (in Aramaic) a רַבִּי *(rabbi)* "ruler, officer or chief" (Dan 2:28).

The term רַב *(rav)* simply means "much", "many", "numerous" or "great." But with the addition of the letter י *(yud)* on the end, a suffix of possession, we can literally translate רַבִּי (rabbi) as "my great one".

It was a general title of respect that recognized that someone has much to offer.

PRAYER: *You are a Teacher to us all; the young, the aged, the inexperienced, and the seasoned. The wise and the simple, all find their need in you, LORD. You are the God of all worlds who reigns on high. You look down upon your progeny and speak kind wisdom into the hearts, and souls that would receive your words.*

The great "I AM" shares his living words and the measure of his greatness with those to whom he entrusts their understanding. Oh, what an awesome calling - to be called, to resound and repeat the wisdom and the council of the LORD to others, to relate his teaching. And just to think, you LORD, have placed us all in this position by charging us to recite and sing your words aloud.

God's truth can come from mouths of babes, stones can cry out if need be, but blessed is a teacher who can learn from the Master of All and from the experience of those who went before him. Do not allow us LORD to fall into the temptation that our intellects and not your Spirit reveals the deep truths of life, that our greatness, theological education, and academic skill are to account for the good in this world because without you, God, we are nothing.

DAY 14 – LOVE

SCRIPTURE: *You shall love the LORD your God with all your heart and with all your soul and with all your might (Deuteronomy 6:5). You shall not take vengeance, nor bear any grudge against the sons of your people, but you shall love your neighbor as yourself; I am the LORD (Leviticus 19:18).*

As it was customary to ask great teachers for wisdom, once Jesus was asked to articulate the greatest of all commandments. He answered without any hesitation.

Jesus, just like Rabbi Hillel before him, affirmed that both greatest commandments were the ones that commanded to love. In the first, love was to be directed towards perfect God, and in the other, love was to be extended to his imperfect people.

Loving people is not easy. In Hebrew לאהוב *(leahov)* means "to love" and אַהֲבָה *(ahavah)* is a noun for "love". What is intriguing is that in Hebrew "liking" and "loving" is the same. To love means to like, and to like, means to love. In many languages there is a clear distinction between "liking" and "loving", but not in Hebrew, אַהֲבָה *(ahavah)* is an all-encompassing idea.

As we ponder God's commandment to love, all kinds of people come across our minds, some we like a lot, others we tolerate, while there could be some we can't stand at all.

Are we truly commanded to love everyone or just some people? Leviticus 19:18 commands us to treat "brothers" fairly and to love "our neighbor" as oneself. The word רֵעַ *(reah)* translated as "neighbor" in Hebrew literally means "someone who is nearby", standing not far from us.

People generally have a notion that if we feel good about someone (we like them) we will do good to them (we will love them). However, according to ancient Eastern wisdom, it is the other way around: If we do good to someone, we also begin to feel good about that person.

PRAYER: *Oh, how you loved us, Lord of Hosts, creator of the ages. For truly we are loved from the very moment of creation. When you made the sky and clouds full of fresh air, and the flowers to produce a sweet aroma, you have loved us. We could have lived in the world so dull and void of beauty, pleasure, and delight, but you have made us able to enjoy so much of this creation we are part of. With everlasting love, you have loved your people even though we've gone astray and separated ourselves from our Maker. Yet, you, Oh, Savior God, in grace chose to withstand the pain we caused you as rebellious creations. In favor, you have brought us back and made a way for us to find you, for those who have strayed so far, even for those who never knew you.*

We praise you, LORD, for your unending love, for the favor that you show towards us, we extol you for your goodness. Through the generations you are good, and we can see your goodness. May we reflect even a part of your goodness and love in our lives to those around us.

DAY 15 – THE GOSPEL

SCRIPTURE: *How lovely on the mountains are the feet of him who brings good news, who announces peace and brings good news of happiness, who announces salvation, and says to Zion, "Your God reigns!" Listen! Your watchmen lift up their voices, they shout joyfully together; for they will see with their own eyes when the LORD restores Zion (Isaiah 52:7-8).*

Various sections of the New Testament were written by Jews living in the Roman Empire sometime in the first century of the Common Era. One of the most important New Testament concepts is εὐαγγέλιον (pronounced: *euangelion*) usually translated in English as "the Gospel". While the word Gospel has a positive connotation in the minds of modern Jesus Christ-followers, most connect it to the life of the Messiah. Yet the Greek word is a translation of Hebrew and this double translation obscures its original meaning.

This Greek word for "gospel" (εὐαγγέλιον; *euangelion*) consists of two words: "good" and "news." To proclaim the Gospel literally means to announce to someone that something good has taken place. In Hebrew, the phrase to proclaim good news is one word - לבשר (pronounced: *levaser*). The word for flesh in Hebrew is בשר *(basar)* and it is possible that לבשר *(levaser)* means "to declare something to people(flesh)". This means that the New Testament idea of the gospel in its original Hebrew framework safeguards us from alienating the "news of good" or "the gospel" to only the spiritual realm.

In ancient times when the armies of Israel faced would-be conquerors, a "messenger" מבשר (pronounced: *mevaser*) much like a modern-day embedded journalist would stand ready to bring home news of defeat or victory. Israel's victories announced that their God came through for his people and was powerful to save them. The armies under the protection of other gods were no match for him.

Hence, when we hear Jesus and Paul proclaim "the Gospel", we must imagine them as the messengers reporting the victorious reign of Israel's God. Jesus' resurrection signals God's triumph over all the enemies of Israel and that is indeed, the news of good (or the good news).

PRAYER: *Mighty King, ruler of all, and master of our very lives, we fall in the presence of your strength. We rejoice in the news that the time is coming when all wrongs will be made right, when all injustices will be eliminated, and you, Lord, our King, will reign from your throne in Jerusalem, the city of your glory.*

Until that day, Oh, God, show us how we can be the messengers of the good news we have heard. Show us how we can spread the news of your reign to the ends of the earth. How blessed are those among us who perceive the seasons when you are near! May we all find the joyful sound we can make to make your creation ready to receive the blessing of good news.

DAY 16 – TOGETHER

SCRIPTURE: *Behold, how good and how pleasant it is for brothers to dwell together in unity! It is like the precious oil upon the head, coming down upon the beard, even Aaron's beard, coming down upon the edge of his robes. It is like the dew of Hermon coming down upon the mountains of Zion; For there the LORD commanded the blessing – life forever (Psalm 133:1-3).*

The words of this Psalm recount the sweetness and delight of worshipping God in the company of others who share so much in common. The Hebrew text uses the term אָחִים *(achim)* to express "brotherhood" and "comradery". As the passage stresses the "goodness" טוֹב *(tov)* also speaks of being together. This "togetherness" is expressed through an interesting root יחד *(yachad)*. It means "being united", or even "united as one".

When someone is "special" or "one of a kind" in modern Hebrew people use the term מאוחד *(meuchad)*. Concepts such as "sole" or "one and only" also have an equivalent connected with the same root יחיד *(yahid)*.

The idea of "unity" best corresponds to a slightly different root in Hebrew - אחד (pronounced: *achad*). For example, in the famous Jewish declaration of faith, the Shema (Deut. 6:4) expresses God's oneness or unity by using this root - שְׁמַע יִשְׂרָאֵל יהוה אֱלֹהֵינוּ יהוה אֶחָד *(shema Yisrael Adonai Eloheinu Adonai echad)* - "Hear, O, Israel, the LORD our God, the LORD is one."

PRAYER: *You are one and your name is one, Almighty. The mystery of your unity is hard to comprehend, yet we walk away with the knowledge that you are unique, one of a kind, and there is no one like you. Many would wish to take your place and wish to be gods, but you are the King of Kings and Master of those who rule, in heaven and on earth.*

We look to you, LORD of Light to unite us, your children, in obedience to you. Yes, we have gone astray and have wandered off from the path of brotherhood too many times to count. Forgive us, Savior for our stubborn will, that we have spurned the dignity of others and have allowed ourselves to stand apart from them as if we are supreme and loftier of creatures. Forgive us, LORD, and bring us back, unite us that we may be one as you are one. May we be found to be worthy children of our Father.

DAY 17 – JACOB & ISRAEL

SCRIPTURE: *Isaac prayed to the LORD on behalf of his wife, because she was barren; and the LORD answered him and Rebekah his wife conceived. But the children struggled together within her; and she said, "If it is so, why then am I this way?" So she went to inquire of the LORD. The LORD said to her, "Two nations are in your womb; And two peoples will be separated from your body; And one people shall be stronger than the other; And the older shall serve the younger." When her days to be delivered were fulfilled, behold, there were twins in her womb. Now the first came forth red, all over like a hairy garment; and they named him Esau. Afterward, his brother came forth with his hand holding on to Esau's heel, so his name was called Jacob (Genesis 25:21-26).*

Jacob's birth name in Hebrew is יַעֲקֹב (pronounced: *Ya'akov*). It is related to the Hebrew word for a "heel" of one's leg - עָקֵב *(akev)*. When baby Esau was being born the midwife could not believe her eyes: his twin brother was holding Esau by his heel, not willing to let him go first! Because of this Rebecca and Isaac called their son the "heel-grabber" - יַעֲקֹב *(Ya'akov)*. Jacob's name defined his life until another unusual event occurred – his personal encounter with a special messenger known in the Bible as the "Angel of the LORD" (Gen.32).

Once again Jacob grabbed and held on tightly to the Angel of the LORD himself as they wrestled. He demanded that he finally be granted a mighty blessing he so greatly valued and passionately desired. Seeing

Jacob's persistence, the Angel of the LORD granted his request by blessing him.

To reflect this new reality in Jacob's life, the Angel gave Jacob a completely new name – יִשְׂרָאֵל *(Yisra'el)* "Israel". The key to understanding Jacob's new name is hidden in the original Hebrew. (Jewish Studies for Christians also published my book called "The Hidden Story of Jacob: What We Can See in Hebrew That We Cannot See in English". Make sure to get it on Amazon.com)

The word is related to the verb לִשְׂרוֹת (pronounced: *lisrot*) which in Biblical Hebrew means to "struggle", to "strive", and even to "exercise influence". In this context, it has to do so with God himself. (Gen 32:30)

Jacob's decedents will forever be known as the people of Israel, the people that struggle with God.

PRAYER: Oh, *God of Israel, you are known as a stronghold of Abraham, as a well of life for Isaac, and a rock for Jacob in the days gone by. You do not cast away your sons who wrestle with your will, those who are free to choose and persevere. Do not let go of us as we hold tight to you, and grant us LORD success in the lives we live on earth. Grant us the prosperity of Abraham; the fruitfulness of our father as we walk in his steps. Oh, teach us, LORD, to be the children worthy of our fathers with whom you forged a bond so long ago. And guide us from the evil which we know is lurking in the shadows, God. Protect your children each day as we reach out for your embrace. Father of Mercy, hear our call and touch us gently now.*

DAY 18 – YESHUA

SCRIPTURE: *And Joseph her husband, being a righteous man and not wanting to disgrace her, planned to send her away secretly. But when he had considered this, behold, an angel of the Lord appeared to him in a dream, saying, "Joseph, son of David, do not be afraid to take Mary as your wife; for the Child who has been conceived in her is of the Holy Spirit. She will bear a Son; and you shall call His name Jesus, for He will save His people from their sins." (Matthew 1:19-21)*

The name Jesus is an English rendering of the New Testament's Ἰησοῦς (pronounced: *Iesoos*) which is a Judeo-Greek adaptation of the Biblical Hebrew name Joshua (יְהוֹשֻׁעַ). It comes to the New Testament via the Septuagint, the Judeo-Greek translation of the Hebrew Bible abbreviated as LXX). The Septuagint is a magnificent work, a result of many years of scrupulous translation from a wide variety of Israelite texts, from the best-known Hebrew manuscripts (at the time), many of which were older than the ones used in traditional Jewish Masoretic texts.

Best scholars can tell LXX was translated by Jewish sages in the Egyptian city of Alexandria long before the first gospel account was ever written down. Because the Septuagint was the most trusted and authoritative Jewish translation available in the first century CE, the New Testament often quotes from the Septuagint. In fact, it is in this Judeo-Greek version of the Hebrew Bible, used by hundreds of thousands of Jews before and during the time of Jesus, where one finds the use of the Greek adaptation word Ἰησοῦς *(Iesoos)* to translate the Hebrew name יְהוֹשֻׁעַ (pronounced: *Yehoshua*). Jesus was called a shortened version of this name - ישוע *(Yeshua)* which mean "salvation" in Hebrew.

So Greek name Ἰησοῦς *(Iesoos)* is a transliteration of Hebrew ישוע *(Yeshua)* and knowing that it means "salvation" the words the angel said begin to make sense. We read in Matt. 1:21: "She will bear a son; and you shall call His name Jesus (salvation), for He will save His people from their sins."

Whatever language we may choose to render these words into today, we must always remember that the reason the son of Mary (Mariam) was called Yeshua (Jesus) is his mission - he was to save his people from their sins. Translating Greek back to Hebrew helps us see this passage clearly.

PRAYER: *Master of our souls, compassionate Father, you hold us in the palm of your hand, and nothing can harm us in your care. What is the meaning of such favor and daily salvation from so many evils that you extend to us? Who are we that you shield us as if we were some precious possessions? We know that you have loved us for the sake of your promises and because of your faithfulness to the patriarchs, because of your own righteousness. We are blessed in this tumultuous life to have security and salvation. We feel unworthy that even when troubles are our own doing, you, the Lord is mighty to save. Lord, you are our salvation and hope, and it is to you we look day-to-day for safety and protection. Blessed be your name, the Lord who saves.*

DAY 19 – ARMIES

SCRIPTURE: *Now it came about when Joshua was by Jericho, that he lifted up his eyes and looked, and behold, a man was standing opposite him with his sword drawn in his hand, and Joshua went to him and said to him, "Are you for us or for our adversaries?" He said, "No; rather I indeed come now as captain of the host of the LORD." And Joshua fell on his face to the earth, and bowed down, and said to him, "What has my lord to say to his servant?" The captain of the LORD'S host said to Joshua, "Remove your sandals from your feet, for the place where you are standing is holy." And Joshua did so (Joshua 5:13-15).*

A famous hymn "A Mighty Fortress is our God" (translated from its original German in old, but still comprehensible English) says, "Did we in our own strength confide, our striving would be losing; were not the right Man on our side, the Man of God's own choosing: Dost ask who that may be? Christ Jesus, it is He; Lord Sabaoth, His name, from age to age the same, and He must win the battle."

Whether in a hymnal or in a Bible translation this unusual title, "Lord Sabaoth" has caused some confusion. I once heard an otherwise a very-well educated worship leader exhorting the congregation by saying that the Lord Sabaoth simply means "the Lord of the Sabbath!" Nothing can be further from the truth (Well some things can be, but as you know, this a common way to say that "I think this is all wrong".)

The Hebrew term is יהוה צְבָאוֹת *(Adonai tsevaot)* and it is not related to the Sabbath at all. In Isaiah 6 the great prophet heard angels call out to each other קָדוֹשׁ קָדוֹשׁ קָדוֹשׁ יהוה צְבָאוֹת - "Holy, Holy, Holy is Adodai Tsevaot".

The Hebrew noun צְבָאוֹת *(tsevaot)* comes from the root which means an "army" or a "multitude", thus a more literal translation would be the "LORD of the Armies".

Nothing illustrates this title better than the story from Joshua Chapter 5, when Joshua met the messenger of the LORD. When Joshua first saw this great warrior, he inquired if the warrior was "for them" (Israel) or "for their enemies". The answer he received was – no. Not letting Joshua wonder too long the heavenly warrior added, "I have come as the Commander of the Army of the LORD". He was שַׂר־צְבָא־יהוה *(sar tsevah Adonai)* the one in charge of the "YHVH's Army"

God of Israel was not satisfied with assisting the national army (fighting on her side). He was intending to lead Israel into battle himself. Joshua immediately understood who stood before him. Just as Moses did before him Joshua fell too facedown and took off his shoes in the presence of the heavenly general.

PRAYER: *Lord of the Armies, God of countless hosts, we do even know all that you command. So much of our own world we have not even seen. Talking about the world that is beyond is even harder to imagine. You truly rule the multitudes of creatures, some of which we have never met or seen. The host of heaven must be filled with life and you've shown glimpses of such things to just a few of us. We seek to be a part of your innumerable host who even now sing praise to who you are in glory. The LORD of the Armies reigns supreme!*

Day 20 – NATIONS

SCRIPTURE: *God be gracious to us and bless us and cause His face to shine upon us - Selah. That Your way may be known on the earth, Your salvation among all nations. Let the peoples praise You, O God; Let all the peoples praise You. Let the nations be glad and sing for joy; For You will judge the peoples with uprightness and guide the nations on the earth. Selah. Let the peoples praise You, O God; let all the peoples praise You (Psalm 67:1-5).*

In Hebrew "nations" is גּוֹיִם *(goim)*, the same word which is often gets translated as "gentiles" into English. Typically Bible uses this term גּוֹיִם *(goim)* to refer to people who are not Israel. Interestingly, when God called Abram to go to the land that one day would be called the Land of Israel, he promised him that he would become a great nation גּוֹי גָּדוֹל *(goy gadol)*. You see God's promise to Abram included not just future Israel but other nations as well.

God said that through Abram, all the other מִשְׁפְּחֹת הָאֲדָמָה *(mishpechot ha'adamah)* "families of the earth" would be blessed (Gen.12:1-3). This is where the "nations" גּוֹיִם *(goim)* come into play. When we read the New Testament or the Hebrew Bible translated into Greek (Septuagint) we see that this term was translated as ἔθνη *(ethnei)*.

When Jesus was brought to the temple as a child one priest was filled with God's spirit and recognized him by saying "my eyes have seen your salvation… a light for revelation to the Gentiles (Nations), and for glory to your people Israel." (Luke 2:30-32). He called Yeshua (Jesus) "light of the nations" אוֹר גּוֹיִם *(ohr goim)* most likely referring to the promise in Isaiah 49:6.

The promise of nations turning to Israel's God is firm and true.

PRAYER: *Worthy of praise and adoration are you, Master of ages. LORD, you have made this world so diverse. In your mercy, you had favor on Noah and his family. In your grace you allowed humans to grow into many families upon this earth. You have chosen Israel to be your special people, but you have not forgotten other nations in this world.*

You have allowed so many cultures to grow and flourish that someday they may find a way to worship you through their own unique songs or dances. You have given the nations their purposes and callings. May all families of the earth can be one because the only way to find true unity is first to be united with you, Oh, King. Be exalted, Oh God in the heavens and here on earth, in the hearts of the people you made for your pleasure.

DAY 21 – ARMAGEDDON

SCRIPTURE: *And I saw coming out of the mouth of the dragon and out of the mouth of the beast and out of the mouth of the false prophet, three unclean spirits like frogs; for they are spirits of demons, performing signs, which go out to the kings of the whole world, to gather them together for the war of the great day of God, the Almighty. ("Behold, I am coming like a thief. Blessed is the one who stays awake and keeps his clothes, so that he will not walk about naked and men will not see his shame"). And they gathered them together to the place which in Hebrew is called Har-Magedon (Revelation 16:13-16).*

The word "Armageddon" comes from the Greek New Testament, its origin is Hebrew. The Hebrew word מְגִדּוֹן *(megidon)* is uncertain in meaning. In fact, it is a geographical location, הַר מְגִדּוֹ *(har megido)* translates as "Mount of Meggido" (Rev.16:16). Armageddon is basically two Hebrew words spelled together in Greek. It is a real place, a multi-layered artificial hill, an old fortress (relatively small portions of which are still in existence) which was used by King Solomon to guard the northern borders of his kingdom.

There are more words like that in English. For example, in the Greek language "Capernaum" does not mean anything, but if you spell it in Hebrew it becomes obvious that it refers to "Nahum's village" - כְּפַר-נָחוּם *(kfar Nachum).*

PRAYER: *LORD, you are the sovereign of order and chaos, of the heights and the lowest parts too, the one who sets things from the beginning and announces to his servants what will take place* *in the end. Master, you called us to walk the path of truth, faith, and reliance on you. When evil comes we should not lose heart, but trust and press on our way, for who can know what we avoid by knowing what's ahead?. you LORD mold our path and order the steps of those who seek your will and listen when you speak. Chaos is scary, uncertainty is something most seek to avoid, but we know the God of order can be found in the most chaotic of circumstances. Let us learn to incline our ears to hear your voice in the stillness of the moment.*

DAY 22 – TORAH

SCRIPTURE: *Hear, my son, your father's instruction and do not forsake your mother's teaching (תורת אמך). Indeed, they are a graceful wreath to your head and ornaments about your neck (Proverbs 1:8-9).*

As people read these verses, the word Torah (is not what usually comes to their minds as they consider mother's teaching/*torah*). The Hebrew word תּוֹרָה (pronounced: *torah*) most often recognized as the Hebrew title for the Five Books of Moses. The term תּוֹרָה *(torah)* actually means "teaching". The root of the word comes from the verb לִירוֹת (pronounced: *lirot*), which illustrates the idea of hitting a target while throwing or shooting something. When the writer of Proverbs tells us not to abandon "mother's teaching", it literally says "your mother's Torah" (תּוֹרַת אִמֶּךָ).

The wisdom and truth about God and His world is dispensed not just by those who have professional qualifications in theology or law, philosophy or ethics, but also (if not primarily) by wise and capable fathers and mothers.

To neglect what parents tell us is a sign of a bigger problem. A person who neglects their parent's instructions will often go on to reject God's teaching as well.

PRAYER: *You LORD is the shepherd of the flock, the guide of the perplexed. You are infinite in wisdom and ability to direct our paths for a good life. In your abundant and sacrificial love,* *you teach us the meaning of love and faithfulness, LORD. By your commitment to the lost and hurting, broken, and downcast you show us the priorities of true mercy, compassion, and strength. Your strength is not found in muscle, nor armies, or weapons, but in your ability to be compassionate and show kindness to the least in this world, even when we are undeserving.*

Almighty, you have given us your teaching, your instructions, and have pointed out the way of life for us so many times. You have set up road signs and monuments to show us the right direction, to remind us about your precepts and principles of truth that never fail. How many times have we aimed to please you, Master, but missed the mark entirely? We bow our knees before you Father, bend our necks, and humble our hearts in awe to you the LORD of Hosts. Lead us each day and help us listen to your voice and follow its directions.

DAY 23 – RAINBOW

SCRIPTURE: *God said, "This is the sign of the covenant which I am making between Me and you and every living creature that is with you, for all successive generations; I set My bow in the cloud, and it shall be for a sign of a covenant between Me and the earth… When the bow is in the cloud, then I will look upon it, to remember the everlasting covenant between God and every living creature of all flesh that is on the earth." And God said to Noah, "This is the sign of the covenant which I have established between Me and all flesh that is on the earth" (Genesis 9:12-13, 16-17).*

Rainbows are majestically colorful. The Hebrew word for rainbow is קֶשֶׁת (pronounced: *keshet*). But קֶשֶׁת *(keshet)* also means a "bow" - the weapon used to propel arrows. We can see a limited connection between a rainbow and a bow even in English. In Hebrew, however, the word is the same, and connection is simply unavoidable.

Let's investigate this connection a little deeper. When God judged the fallen humanity by sending a catastrophe, a flood, he made Noah a very important promise. God said that he would not judge the world in this manner again.

A rainbow became an eternal sign and a symbol of God's forgiveness and his covenantal faithfulness. God's bow of war is now hanged up on permanent display pointing to heaven and away from us. Yet this sign of mercy and faithfulness is also a reminder that we are not free to cause whatever moral havoc we wish. It is true that God has promised never again to send this kind of catastrophic flood to earth, He has not promised to fully disengage from seeing and judging the evil that fills our world.

PRAYER: *God of Creation, Lord of Hosts, you have set the lights in the sky, you created a great diversity of plants, animals, fish, and all manner of life. You command the seas, the tides, and the clouds. You even ordered all the languages of men. We know did not always honor you as the King and Creator. People can forget their Maker in their rebellion. You had to destroy the world you made for us with water, but then you graced us with your rainbow, a promise of your favor, we were blessed with a burst of light color.*

No, Savior, we cannot comprehend the depth of your great wisdom no matter how long we drink the waters from your wells of Salvation. Yet we never grow satisfied, always seeking more, always hungry for greater understanding, oh, Provider. You always bring redemption, LORD, you seek to be known by us since the days when Adam walked with you in Eden. If we could know today, Oh, God Most High, the glimpses of the plan you have for us and our children we probably would dance as David danced before you. Be praised, Creator of all in majesty above, as we recite your praises day and night.

DAY 24 – HOLY

SCRIPTURE: *In the year of King Uzziah's death I saw the LORD sitting on a throne, lofty and exalted, with the train of His robe filling the temple. Seraphim stood above Him, each having six wings: with two he covered his face, and with two he covered his feet, and with two he flew. And one called out to another and said, "Holy, Holy, Holy, is the LORD of hosts, The whole earth is full of His glory" (Isaiah 6:1-3).*

Isaiah saw the angels calling out to each other: "Holy, Holy, Holy is the Lord God Almighty. The whole Earth is full of his glory!" What an amazing vision this must have been. In traditional Jewish worship, these verses are recounted each day, as each person who prays seeks to join their voice with the praises of the heavenly host.

But why did angels sing of God's holiness and what is so remarkable about that? In Hebrew, the word קָדוֹשׁ (pronounced *kadosh*) translates as "holy" or "set apart".

That the word was repeated several times is important (קָדוֹשׁ קָדוֹשׁ קָדוֹשׁ) – a common way to emphasize something in Hebrew. The essence of holiness is the idea of "being other" or "different" in the sense of being set apart and being able to be compared with anyone or anything. Holy is the exact opposite of something that common, ordinary, and familiar.

Sometimes things, places, and even people can be called holy. The holiest room in the tablercanle was called קֹדֶשׁ הַקֳּדָשִׁים *(kodesh hakodeshim)*, sometimes translated "holy of holies" (Ex 26:33).

Only YHVH alone possesses the absolute holiness. Everything and everyone else is deemed holy by association only because YHVH touches it.

PRAYER: *LORD God Almighty in your strength who can compare with you? There is no limit to your power, no end to what you do with your right hand as you decide to show yourself amidst your people. You are mighty to rescue and mighty to comfort, you cause your glory to shine upon us. You are mighty to judge and to crush those who rebel, you are mighty to silence the wicked and lift up the afflicted. You are holy; you stand apart from all your creation. Nothing in this world compares to you, because you are totally other in your holiness and grace.*

We join our voices to the host of heaven that proclaim your holiness as they continually acclaim your majestic attributes. Look upon us, Oh, God of salvation and might, Holy God, and find favor in the worship of your children. Endow us with a portion of your holiness so we may demonstrate it throughout the world. Be lifted on the throne of your glory, and in our praises today and forever.

DAY 25 – JUDAH

SCRIPTURE: *I saw in the right hand of Him who sat on the throne a book written inside and on the back, sealed up with seven seals. And I saw a strong angel proclaiming with a loud voice, "Who is worthy to open the book and to break its seals?" And no one in heaven or on the earth or under the earth was able to open the book or to look into it. Then I began to weep greatly because no one was found worthy to open the book or to look into it; and one of the elders said to me, "Stop weeping; behold, the Lion that is from the tribe of Judah, the Root of David, has overcome so as to open the book and its seven seals" (Revelation 5:1-5).*

This passage depicts the glorious Messiah as the "Root of David" and the "Lion from the tribe of Judah". The word יְהוּדָה *(Yehudah)* is usually translated as "Judah" in English Bibles, a person's name. While the importance of Judah (one of the sons of Jacob) is obvious the meaning of the name only comes alive in Hebrew.

The name comes from a Hebrew verb לְהוֹדוֹת (pronounced: *lehodot)*, which means "to thank". In the context of the Hebrew Bible, such thanks are synonymous not just with gratitude, but also with praise.

In fact, there was a particular sacrifice called "the sacrifice of thanksgiving" which in the Jerusalem Temple was called תּוֹדָה (pronounced: *todah*) sacrifice – "thanksgiving." In Modern Hebrew, תּוֹדָה *(todah)* is a way we say "thank you."

The name Judah is related to "thanksgiving" and "praise" (Gen 29:35). In fact, the English word "Jews" יְהוּדִים *(yehudim)* simply means "people of Judah" or more literally "people who praise".

PRAYER: *Thank you, Father, that you promised to give to those who seek, to open to those who knock, to not withhold good from those who ask. We are thankful to you for who you are. We come before you, Oh, God, with requests and with so many needs, for we are truly needy. We have many needs, but most of all, we are poor in spirit, LORD, and need deep discernment to perceive your will for us each day. We have studied your council, your laws, your decrees, your instruction in holiness, but there is always more.*

We strive, Oh, Almighty to do what is right, to take the right turns, to walk the narrow paths, but we desperately need more light and to hear your voice as we make our way forward. We seek to be people who praise you, whose lips never stop to utter thanks to you, our God. The one who made us, the one who fashioned us, and the one who molds us as clay is able to restore justice and bring the nations of the world under the banner of his reign. Your mercy endures forever!

DAY 26 – HEBREW

SCRIPTURE: *By faith Abraham, when he was tested, offered up Isaac, and he who had received the promises was offering up his only begotten son; it was he to whom it was said, "IN ISAAC YOUR DESCENDANTS SHALL BE CALLED." He considered that God is able to raise people even from the dead, from which he also received him back as a type (Hebrews 11:17-19).*

Before the people of Israel were known as "Jews" (that name became popular after return from Babylon) the Bible referred to them as "Hebrews". The first "Hebrew" was Abraham. What does the Bible mean by calling him "Hebrew"? The word "Hebrew" comes from the verb לַעֲבוֹר (pronounced: *la'avor*), which means "to cross over" which at first seems strange, but then things become clear.

Abraham crossed over from Mesopotamia (modern-day Iraq) into Canaan (modern day Israel). Abraham crossed over from the world of idol worship familiar to him and his family, into a new realm (where One true God was worshiped instead). In both senses, Abraham forever became an עִבְרִי *(ivri)* – "one who has crossed over".

From the stand point of the indigenous people the one who crossed over from another place is still a foreigner now living in their land.

Eventually, his entire family became known by such name and this name became their primary identity.

When they grew into a large clan they became known as "children of Israel" and only much later "Jews".

Today, all who believe in one God repeat the journey of Abraham. They may not need to cross over from idol-worship. Many people today are born into societies that no longer worship statues and myriads of gods. But to follow one true God they must cross over from death to life, from darkness to light, from sin to righteousness. Since majority of people do not come from believing backgrounds, they will always be considered by the majority to be "foreigners living among them". In some way every serious Christ-follower is a Hebrew.

PRAYER: *Merciful Father, Author of Life, we are so grateful you call out to us. If you did not reveal yourself to us, would we even know you? If you did not show I the truth would we even know right from wrong? If you did not allow us to know about you we may have never found you on our own and walked in darkness and confusion without end. Now that we know who you are, now that we have seen your works, have tasted your provision we will follow you anywhere. You called Abram to follow you to an unknown land and he crossed over and so do we today. We cross over to your side, to the land you have prepared for us.*

Give us ears that are inclined to the sound of your still small voice and help us avert disastrous roads. Thank you for hearing the prayers of your people.

DAY 27 – HALLELUIAH

SCRIPTURE: *Praise the LORD! Praise the name of the LORD; Praise Him, O servants of the LORD, You who stand in the house of the LORD, In the courts of the house of our God! Praise the LORD, for the LORD, is good; Sing praises to His name, for it is lovely. For the LORD has chosen Jacob for Himself, Israel for His own possession (Psalm 135:1-4).*

Who does not know or have not heard the word Halleluiah? It seems that everyone, even non-religious people understand this word as some sort of joyful exclamation. The word sounds pretty much the same in most languages, and for a good reason. Whether it is pronounced in English, or German, or Spanish, or Russian, the word "Halleluiah" is Hebrew loanword. It does not have an independent and unique meaning in those languages, because it was borrowed from ancient Hebrew.

In Hebrew Halleluiah is actually two words, it's a short phrase. The first part is a verb הַלְלוּ *(halelu)* "you praise" which speaks in a command voice. The second part of the word is a short form of God's special name – יָה *(yah)*. In Jewish tradition that stems from deep antiquity. God's special name יהוה *(yhvh)* is never vocalized in full, so it makes sense that it would be abbreviated.

It is quite appropriate to translate the term Halleluiah (הַלְלוּ יָה) as "Praise ("ye", using old English) the LORD".

The Hebrew Bible is full of language that directs us to praise God, but what many people fail to see in English is that it directs us to praise God as a community, to do so together with others. We often fail to see why that is important. Praising God together with other people binds us as a community, as people who have a shared experience of God.

PRAYER: *We praise you, Oh, King, we lift-up your name in this world for all to know who you are. The sound of your name sends enemies into a chaotic panic. The weight of it causes us to fall on our knees. We cannot help but fall before you, LORD God. We find salvation in your name alone and there is no other name in the world that can do such great deeds. But your name is not mere sounds or letters, or a song; it's not numbers or syllables uttered in some specific order. Your name is your essence, it is who you are, what you do, how we know you, and see you today.*

We praise you for the breath of life, LORD. We do not take it for granted because nothing in this world is guaranteed. We praise you in the presence of others, Master of All. Redeemer, King, and mighty fortress are you, God. The Righteous may find shelter, safety, and protection within your walls. The weak look to you for support and the strong turn to you for guidance. You are the Prince of Peace and a mighty warrior.

Are we short of reasons to praise your name, God? Who else deserves the praise but you? We worship at your throne.

DAY 28 – PENTECOST

SCRIPTURE: *When the day of Pentecost had come, they were all together in one place. And suddenly there came from heaven a noise like a violent rushing wind, and it filled the whole house where they were sitting. And there appeared to them tongues as of fire distributing themselves, and they rested on each one of them. And they were all filled with the Holy Spirit and began to speak with other tongues, as the Spirit was giving them utterance. Now there were Jews living in Jerusalem, devout men from every nation under heaven... (Acts 2:1-5)*

One of the three most important feasts of Israel is Shavuot (שבועות), which literally means "weeks" in Hebrew שבוע means "a week", and ות is a plural feminine ending. The festival is called "Weeks" because its date is determined by counting off seven weeks just after Passover. The practice is called "counting of the Omer".

In keeping with the age-old Hellenistic Jewish Tradition, the Septuagint translated "Shavuot" as "Pentecost" (Πεντηκοστὴ), which literally means 50 or 50th, signifying seven weeks plus one more day. Shavuot in the Hebrew Bible was a festival of agricultural blessing - God's provision of food to Israel. The Shavuot/Pentecost of Acts 2, along with its echo among Gentile God-fearers in Acts 10 is a defining once-in-a-lifetime event when the Holy Spirit becomes the ultimate provision of spiritual substance to God's people. In later Jewish tradition, however, Shavuot is firmly connected to the giving of the Torah. It is intriguing that none of the Biblical references to

Shavuot (Ex. 34:22 and Deut. 16:10) and its alternative names - Festival of Reaping (Ex. 23:16) or the Day of the First Fruits (Num. 29:26) even hint at the giving of Torah to Israel.

It is clear that by the first century CE there were already some connections made with the reception of Torah on Shavuot (Jub. 6:15-22). But these later cultural traditions became the focus only after the Jewish people entered exile and could no longer observe the agricultural aspects of the festival, working their own land.

When we trust God, from one week to another, when we dedicate ourselves to trusting in his bounty, he provides for us just what we need on every level, spiritually and physically. We must never forget that what we have are gifts and God deserves our gratitude.

PRAYER: *God of Creation, maker of all, you created the heavenly bodies and set your seasons in their place. Enable us to rejoice in the fruits of the land and find satisfaction the results of our labors that we may praise you from the depth of our souls. We delight in thoughts of the age to come. But it is hard to comprehend eternity, for everything in our world is finite and appears to have a beginning and an end. Thank you, Eternal Father, for giving us awareness of our limits and for revealing to us your eternal plans and purposes. You give us gifts and feed us and sustain us. We praise you because all we have comes from you. Embolden us with your spirit to proclaim your greatness throughout the world.*

DAY 29 – NISSI

SCRIPTURE: *Then the LORD said to Moses, "Write this in a book as a memorial and recite it to Joshua, that I will utterly blot out the memory of Amalek from under heaven." Moses built an altar and named it The LORD is My Banner; and he said, "The LORD has sworn; the LORD will have war against Amalek from generation to generation." (Exodus 17:14-16)*

There is a very peculiar name for God in the Bible יהוה נִסִּי (*Adonai Nissi*). Moses called God by this very name when He gave Israel victory over the Amalekites in the wilderness in Ex. 17:15. Most English Bible translations render it as the "LORD is my Banner", basically communicating the idea of a flag of some sort.

In ancient Hebrew, the word נֵס (*nes*) can mean a "flag", but also a "sign", or an "ensign" (Jer. 51:12; Is. 49:22). Moreover, the word נִסִּי *(nissi)* "my banner" is connected by its root to the verb לָשֵׂאת *(laset)* which means to "carry", to "lift", to "raise up". This Hebrew verb נָשָׂא *(nasa)* is very common and relates both "an upward motion" and "carrying", which makes perfect sense in the context of a banner or a sign. When the sons of Korah were killed in. In Num 26:10 we read that they וַיִּהְיוּ לְנֵס *(vayihyu lanes)* "became as a warning sign" to those who watched their demise.

In Num. 21:8, Moses set a bronze serpent on a נֵס *(nes)* which most Bibles render as a "pole". In that sense, the word was not meant as a flag or a banner, but was used idiomatically as a "miracle", a "supernatural sign". This is exactly how the word is used in Modern Hebrew today.

We must look deeper into this unusual name of God and recognize that the mighty banner of the Lord which is lifted high upon the earth, draws all to his glory, his love, and salvation. The name יהוה נִסִּי (*Adonai Nissi*) – *"The LORD is My Banner"* is a sign in and of itself, a miracle, a testimony of his glorious deeds.

PRAYER: *Mighty God, worker of wonders, you lift our heads from day to day and sustain us with your strength. To you we look and in you we hope as the world around us is oblivious to your sustaining power, deceived by notions of self-reliance. Give us eyes to see your signs in all of your creation, and your miracles, no matter how small they may appear. Do not let us remain unaware. Nothing in this world happens by chance and things that occur have a purpose.*

Aid us, Oh, Lord, to recognize your signs, to see the banner of your ever-present glory lifted high about all the nations of the world. Just as you lifted the truth in days past, may our generation find favor in your eyes to be worthy of your revelation of your might. Do not forsake even the most blinded among us, Oh, God, and lift your banner high for all to notice, so that the world may know you as well as your mercy and kindness before the day of reckoning.

DAY 30 – SHALOM

SCRIPTURE: *The LORD bless you, and keep you; The LORD make His face shine on you, And be gracious to you; The LORD lift up His countenance on you, And give you peace' (Numbers 6:24-26).*

We all yarn for peace, on a personal level, in our families, countries and across the entire globe. The Hebrew word שָׁלוֹם *(shalom)* is usually translated as "peace", but this translation is not very precise. As well-known as this word may be the common translation into English severely limits us from seeing its full depth. This is where looking deeper into Hebrew brings forth understanding, treasures, and wisdom.

Hebrew is a root language and much can be uncovered by looking at related words. It turns out that שָׁלוֹם *(shalom)* is connected with such verbs as לְהַשְׁלִים *(lehashlim)* and לְשַׁלֵּם *(leshalem)* which range in meaning from "to make a payment" to "to make whole" and "to fulfill that which is lacking".

YHVH in Jewish Christ not only grants us peace, but he also makes us complete. He fulfills us in inner workings that we do not understand. In fact, because we are sinful and imperfect the Father of Mercies settles the bill on our behalf (you know, the old, old story). The price we owe is far too high for us to pay without the overwhelming and undeserved grace and mercy of our God.

PRAYER: *Almightily God, who makes peace in the high places, make peace for us all. We yearn for peace LORD, genuine peace that can only endure when the King reigns in the hearts of men who fear him. We know, oh, God, that all men desire tranquility but for different reasons. Our ambitions are deep and our ways are sometimes far from yours. We can desire something good but in the most selfish way. LORD, you are just, and you test your servants, whether we are peacemakers and truly fear heaven or wicked tenants concerned with amassing power and gaining things in this world.*

God, you test us in our walk of righteousness so often. You give, and you take away. You watch from on high how we respond to you, to things that happen in our lives whether it be faithfulness or indignation. Master help us keep our hearts humble, our ways upright, our souls pure and not given to evil inclinations. Lead us not into temptation and teach us how to pursue peace with all men. We wish to be complete and realize that we can only be complete in you!

DAY 31 – ZION

SCRIPTURE: *How blessed is everyone who fears the LORD, Who walks in His ways. When you shall eat of the fruit of your hands, You will be happy and it will be well with you. Your wife shall be like a fruitful vine Within your house, Your children like olive plants Around your table. Behold, for thus shall the man be blessed Who fears the LORD. The LORD bless you from Zion, and may you see the prosperity of Jerusalem all the days of your life. Indeed, may you see your children's children. Peace be upon Israel! (Psalm. 128:1-6)*

A Biblical Hebrew name that people often associate with Jerusalem, with God's holy abode, with his special mountain is mount Zion. In Hebrew, it is צִיוֹן (pronounced: *tziyon*). Because we are familiar with the word and simply think of it as a proper name, we forget that it has concrete meaning. Like most, if not all, names in Hebrew names it can tell an interesting story.

This is where translations and transliterations from Hebrew do not help us but looking closely at their roots does. The word Zion appears to come from the verb לְצַיֵּן *(letzayen)*, which means "to mark something" or in modern Hebrew use "to emphasize something".

Could it be that the word Zion means "a mark", a place, a location which was chosen? It may not sound very special or spiritual until we think who made the mark.

PRAYER: *Adonai Tzidkenu, LORD our Righteousness, may you be blessed from Zion forever. You have set up a seat of* *your glory on your holy mountain in Judea. You have chosen a place for your name to dwell on top of Moriah. Master, you have built Jerusalem as a city of your kings, the refuge for those who run to you. In righteousness and holiness, you reign from your throne in Zion and the glory of your house is esteemed all over the world. For generations the city lay in ruins, but it is alive and full of your people once again, for your sons and daughters have returned as you promised so long ago.*

You marked these mountains, these valleys, these streets with your special touch and allowed your presence to dwell amidst the people behind the veil. LORD, we yearn for the days spoken by the prophets when your holy place will be restored and men from many nations will be drawn to Zion, to your city to worship you, oh, King, in your temple. Praise be to you, Oh, LORD, for restoring Zion in our day, for allowing us to see glimpses of your coming. May we never lose the sight to see things unseen, a spiritual sight to see what is not yet but is coming.

DAY 32 – YIREH

SCRIPTURE: *Isaac spoke to Abraham his father and said, "My father". And he said, "Here I am, my son". And he said, "Behold, the fire and the wood, but where is the lamb for the burnt offering?" Abraham said, "God will provide for Himself the lamb for the burnt offering, my son". So the two of them walked on together. Then Abraham raised his eyes and looked, and behold, behind him a ram caught in the thicket by his horns; and Abraham went and took the ram and offered him up for a burnt offering in the place of his son. Abraham called the name of that place The LORD Will Provide, as it is said to this day, "In the mount of the LORD it will be provided" (Gen. 22:7-8, 13-14).*

It is not a secret that God has many names in the Bible. In Gen 22:14 Abram called a particular place where he experienced God - "the LORD will provide". This can be one of those names ascribed to God - יהוה יִרְאֶה (pronounced: *adonai[1] yireh*). Following the special covenant named for God (יהוה) is יִרְאֶה *(yireh)* a word that comes from the verb לִרְאוֹת *(lirot)* "to see, to perceive, to look".

This same root is used to describe someone who has the ability to see things that others cannot. In Hebrew, a רֹאֶה (pronounced: *roeh*) is a "prophet" or a "seer". There is another Biblical Hebrew term - רָאָה פָנֶה *(ra'ah paneh)* - a person who literally "looks into the face". It usually translates as an "advisor" or "overseer".

---

[1] Here we followed a standard Jewish practice of replacing the too-holy-to-pronounce covenant name of God with less holy alternative that is generally approved for common pronunciation.

There is a reason why many English Bibles translate Jehovah Jireh *(YHVH yhireh)* "The LORD will provide" even if Hebrew says something else. The Hebrew phrase literally says "LORD will see/see to it".

While the idea of "providing" versus "seeing/seeing to it" is not identical, they are not too far off in ancient Hebrew. In Gen. 22 the verb is used several times and God is described as "one who will see to it" or "one who will look out for his interest." Unlike people, when God sees he can give assurances that what he perceives can easily become a reality.

PRAYER: *God of Abundance, you sustain all of us in your mercy. You are the true provider and everything we have comes from your hand. We tend to think of ourselves as working and laboring to achieve results, but we are depending on the stability you establish, on fruits of our labor which will sustain us in life. We expect that the pests will not wipe out our harvest, that the sun will not scorch our fields, and that the clouds will give enough rain. But who commands these into perfect balance? No fruit we have, and no product we produce comes without you first providing the very things needed to make that come about.*

So, thank you, Father, for your provisions, for your generosity in answering our needs, for giving us nature that we learn from day to day. Thank you, Holy One, for giving to us beyond our daily needs, so much abundance that we can share with others. We return to you our gratitude and perhaps a portion of our wealth, which you have provided in the first place.

DAY 33 – OBSERVANCE

SCRIPTURE: *Solomon did what was evil in the sight of the LORD, and did not follow the LORD fully, as David his father had done. Then Solomon built a high place for Chemosh the detestable idol of Moab, on the mountain which is east of Jerusalem, and for Molech the detestable idol of the sons of Ammon. Thus also he did for all his foreign wives, who burned incense and sacrificed to their gods. Now the LORD was angry with Solomon because his heart was turned away from the LORD, the God of Israel, who had appeared to him twice, and had commanded him concerning this thing, that he should not go after other gods; but he did not observe what the LORD had commanded. (1 Ki. 11: 6-10).*

People have different ideas when they hear about someone observing or not observing something. In English, the term can bring up associations with looking at something, but not in Hebrew. In this story, the LORD was angry with Solomon because he engaged in idolatry. Solomon knew the living God but put on the show for his wives to honor their foreign deities. In 1 Kings 11:9 when Hebrew texts says "And the LORD was angry with Solomon" it uses the verb יִתְאַנַּף (pronounced: *yitanaph*). This word is connected to the noun for "nose" (אף) because in ancient Hebrew the idea of anger is a picture, an image of someone breathing hard through his/her nose. This is not an attractive picture.

One can see why God would be angry with Solomon. People look up to their king and his behavior was clearly wrong. The text says that Solomon did not observe (לֹא שָׁמַר) what God commanded (v.10). The verb to "observe" שָׁמַר (pronounced: *shamar*) in Hebrew and it also carries an idea of "looking". More precisely it means to "watch" and to "guard" as if something important. It also means to "keep" in a sense of preserving something that is. In Modern Hebrew, שומר (pronounced: *shomer*) means a "watchman" or a "security guard on patrol". But in Biblical Hebrew it means someone who observes or keeps God's commandments.

The idea of keeping, guarding, and being watchful in regards to how we follow God is built into this verb שָׁמַר *(shamar)*. This is exactly what Solomon failed to do. God gave him instructions, but the king did not observe or guard his words and incurred God's anger as a result. God's words should be valuable to us just as a treasure that requires to be kept safe and secure.

PRAYER: *Turn away your anger from us when we fail to keep your commandments. Do not hold us in contempt of your laws Master for we are wayward and flawed in our judgment. We can lose sight that your instructions should be observed and guarded, preserved, and kept safe. But we beseech you, LORD, we beg not for justice, but for mercy. For surely in justice will find our doom. Let your mercy and goodness triumph over the condemnation of the sinners who come in repentance before you, Oh, King. As your subjects, we are unwise to ignore your justified anger and zeal for your holiness. God of Hope, lead us to your light. Return us to yourself and will never depart. With full strength, we will seek to obey your charge to show the intent of our hearts and respect for your boundaries that exist for our own good. We beseech you Oh, God, hold no anger against us this day.*

DAY 34 – GLORY

SCRIPTURE: *Now when Solomon had finished praying, fire came down from heaven and consumed the burnt offering and the sacrifices, and the glory of the LORD filled the house. The priests could not enter into the house of the LORD because the glory of the LORD filled the LORD'S house. All the sons of Israel, seeing the fire come down and the glory of the LORD upon the house, bowed down on the pavement with their faces to the ground, and they worshiped and gave praise to the LORD, saying, "Truly He is good, truly His lovingkindness is everlasting" (2 Chron. 7:1-3).*

The Hebrew word for "glory" is כָּבוֹד (pronounced: *kavod*). Its meaning is encapsulated in its very root. This same Hebrew word is also often translated as "honor" in the Bible. When we are told to honor our parents in ten commandments the Hebrew the same term only as a verb. The general idea of כָּבֵד (pronounced: *kaved*) in Hebrew means "heavy" and "weighty". Therefore, the verb לְכַבֵּד *(lechabed)* "to honor" carries the notion of making something heavy (vs. making something light). In a sense that is what honoring someone means, to consider them and their authority with some considerable weight.

Hebrew shows us something much deeper and concrete than English can reveal. The opposite idea is קָלוֹן (*qalon*) – "shame" or "dishonor" and קַל (*qal*) means "light" (vs. heavy). It may be strange to think of it in such terms, but God's glory is his heaviness, his importance, his substance, his authority, and weight. God's glory filled the space with his weight and the priests were not able to move, so heavy was God's presence in their midst.

PRAYER: *We fall before you, LORD, and in your presence revel before the God of Power, the God of Might, Bright Morning Star, the Lily of the Valleys. The weight of glory falls and overpowers us. Can we withstand the weight of your Spirit in our midst? No Lord, we know that we are not truly worthy of your presence! It is by grace alone that we stand before you as you dwell in courts of praise that we visit to seek an audience with you.*

So take our worship, LORD, take it as acts of reverent service, as we wish to magnify and to increase your praise in all the world. Teach us and show us how to serve you, and when your glory falls on us, we will know that we tried our best not to diminish your renown but instead to increase your glory. We are grateful that we can be in your presence daily, that you do not grow tired of us or our supplications as we seek your presence in our lives.
Blessed be your name, LORD, from the rising of the sun and to its setting. Hear our prayers rise to you and the words of praise from the time we rise to the moment we fall asleep.

DAY 35 – GLOW

SCRIPTURE: *It came about when Moses was coming down from Mount Sinai (and the two tablets of the testimony were in Moses' hand as he was coming down from the mountain), that Moses did not know that the skin of his face shone because of his speaking with Him. So when Aaron and all the sons of Israel saw Moses, behold, the skin of his face shone, and they were afraid to come near him (Ex. 34:29-30).*

When Moses interacted with God face-to-face, he experienced some prolonged effects of being in God's presence. Apparently, his face glowed with shining radiance. Yet when we look at pictorial representations by many medieval artists, we cannot help but notice that in their imagination Moses is often depicted with horns! How did the great artists of the past such as Michelangelo, (among many others), conceive of the idea that Moses had horns on his head? To put it simply - something got lost in translation.

In the English translation of the Latin Vulgate, we read "his face was horned from the conversation of the Lord" (Ex. 34:29). Because ancient Hebrew did not have written vowel marks, the Hebrew verb קרן (pronounced *keren*) was translated into Latin (and later English) as "grown horns" instead of "shining radiance". If the translators know the proper vowels, they would have not made this mistake.

This example shows us how translations can mislead us. Looking into Hebrew and being able to know what is says always allows for greater clarity.

PRAYER: Oh, *King of Wisdom, LORD of All, our hopes rest with you alone. What is our human wisdom and understanding compared to your perfection? We do not even understand each other since the days you have confused our languages at the tower of Babel. Did we deserve the chaos and confusion that you brought upon us by mixing up men's tongues? Alas, we conceived evil in your sight, and we were so bold in our thoughts that we could attain by our effort the renown only you have. In arrogance we sought to place ourselves next to your name and shamed ourselves by trying.*

Forgive us, LORD, and give us of your Spirit now. Restore, at least to some of us, the understanding of your ways, your speech, the depth of tongues you chose to show yourself to men of old. We need to know and understand your words. You have expressed yourself in human language, so give us the ability to learn and to understand the revelation of your grace. May we grasp the language of your revelation, Oh, Lord of Mercy, so that once more, we do not make fools of ourselves in our mistaken ideas. We need to know your words and your will, so that we may follow you in all righteousness.

DAY 36 – HAKIPPURIM

SCRIPTURE: *Be gracious to me, O God, according to Your lovingkindness; According to the greatness of Your compassion blot out my transgressions. Wash me thoroughly from my iniquity and cleanse me from my sin. For I know my transgressions, and my sin is ever before me. Against You, You only, I have sinned and done what is evil in Your sight, so that You are justified when You speak and blameless when You judge… Create in me a clean heart, O God, and renew a steadfast spirit within me. Do not cast me away from Your presence and do not take Your Holy Spirit from me. Restore to me the joy of Your salvation and sustain me with a willing spirit. Then I will teach transgressors Your ways, and sinners will be converted to You (Psalm. 51:1-4, 10-13).*

Once a year the High Priest of Israel entered a place known as the "holy of holies" קֹדֶשׁ הַקֳּדָשִׁים - (pronounced: *kodesh hakodashim*). It was an inner sanctum within the ancient Temple, a place that was defined by its utter holiness. That special day on the Israelite calendar is called יוֹם הַכִּפֻּרִים (pronounced: *yom hakippurim*), which translates into English as the "Day of Atonement" or literally "the day of coverings"

The cover on the Ark of the Covenant - the place where the blood of the sacrifice was sprinkled by the High Priest was located in this special place - the holy of holies. This cover is called in Hebrew כפורת (pronounced: *kaporet*). In that inner room was the epicenter of God's mercy between the wings of the cherubim, the location where sins were atoned for.

We read in Lev. 17:11: "For the life of the flesh is in the blood, and I have given it for you on the altar to (לְכַפֵּר; *lekapher*) to 'atone' for your souls, for it is the blood by reason of the life that (יְכַפֵּר; *yikaper*) 'makes atonement.'" The verb to "atone" (לְכַפֵּר; *lekapher*) and the "cover" of the Ark of the Covenant - כפורת (*kaporet*), as well as the name of this sacred day - יוֹם הַכִּפֻּרִים (*yom hakippurim*) all, come from the same root that expresses the idea of "covering". To atone for sin, therefore means to "cover" it. In the case of sacrifices, it was the blood of the innocent that covered the guilt of sinners. God made a miraculous and gracious provision so that mankind did not have to die for their own sin, by showing mercy through the blood of atonement. A life substituted for another. Yet, until Christ, this sacrifice had to be made annually and continually. Messiah has become the sacrifice of atonement for all who believe and are willing to be washed and purified through his death. This message is no less solemn than that of the Day of Atonement in the ancient Temple.

PRAYER: *Merciful Father, lover of our souls, creator of our very breath, we revel in your holiness and melt in awe of you. You are entirely other, set apart from your creation, yet you desire to dwell in the world and among the people you created. In your perfection, you have charged us to take special care in coming before you. Yet our iniquities and transgressions, our uncleanness and polluted lives can bring sin into your presence which stands apart from all such things. Cover us with the blood of sacrifices, LORD. Atone and cleanse us from the top of our heads to the bottom of our feet as we stand before you, our Master. Cover our transgressions with your mercy, pour out your grace on the hearts that forget to offer praises to you in proper times.*

DAY 37 – IDF

SCRIPTURE: *He who dwells in the shelter of the Most High will abide in the shadow of the Almighty. I will say to the LORD, "My refuge and my fortress, My God, in whom I trust!" For it is He who delivers you from the snare of the trapper And from the deadly pestilence. He will cover you with His pinions, And under His wings you may seek refuge; His faithfulness is a shield and bulwark. You will not be afraid of the terror by night, Or of the arrow that flies by day; Of the pestilence that stalks in darkness, Or of the destruction that lays waste at noon. A thousand may fall at your side and ten thousand at your right hand, But it shall not approach you. You will only look on with your eyes And see the recompense of the wicked For you have made the LORD, my refuge, Even the Most High, your dwelling place. No evil will befall you, Nor will any plague come near your tent (Ps. 91:1-10).*

The words of Psalms often call on God for defense, describing the LORD as a fortress and refuge, a place to hide. Enemies do come to destroy us and defense is what we need most at such moments. Shortly after declaring Israel's Independence, David Ben-Gurion, Israel's Defense Minister and Prime Minister issued the order which established the Israel Defense Forces (IDF). In Hebrew, we call it *tzahal* (צ.ה.ל. or צה"ל) but that is not a proper Hebrew word. It's an acronym for צְבָא הַהֲגָנָה לְיִשְׂרָאֵל *(tzeva hahagana leyisrael)*.

Israel's army was intentionally called a Defence Force because its primary purpose was never seen as an offensive body. The middle word is הגנה *(haganah)* means "defense". It does not appear in the Bible in this form but the verb "to protect" גָּנַן *(ganan)* does. Also גַן (gan) means "garden" (lit. the protected place), while גנן (ganan) also means "gardner" (the protector).

Perhaps a better known and related biblical word is מגן *(magen)* "a shield". In Genesis 15 God came to Abram and told him not to fear as he embarks on an uncertain journey. The Almighty himself will be his shield.

PRAYER: *You are our defense, LORD, a fortress we can run to. You were a shield to Abraham, to Moses, and to David. Your strength cannot be surpassed and if you do not choose to move, no one can shake your foundation, and we find refuge within your walls. When enemies rise up against us we look to you to give us strength for you have promised to hold us in your hand, not to leave us or forsake us. In our deepest distress, we can lean on you, Master of Heavenly Armies. Thank you, LORD, for your promises.*

We will continue to lift up your name as a banner over us, as our battle cry and the ensign for those who know your goodness. Salvation is your name, LORD, and kind mercies are found in your tents, Oh, God. Thank you for being our strength when we have none. Thank you for being our worth when we feel that there is nothing redeemable in us. Thank you for being the example of virtue and goodness to us, a shield to those who place their hope in you.

DAY 38 – KNESSET

SCRIPTURE: *Now the rest of the people, the priests, the Levites, the gatekeepers, the singers, the temple servants and all those who had separated themselves from the peoples of the lands to the law of God, their wives, their sons, and their daughters, all those who had knowledge and understanding, are joining with their kinsmen, their nobles, and are taking on themselves a curse and an oath to walk in God's law, which was given through Moses, God's servant, and to keep and to observe all the commandments of GOD our Lord, and His ordinances and His statutes (Neh. 10:28-29).*

This passage in Nehemiah describes a purposeful coming together of people from various facets of Israeli society. They band together in their commitment to worship God as one, yet when this occurs unity is hard to achieve. You may know that the main legislative body in Israel today is called כנסת (Knesset).

A Jewish place of worship is called בית הכנסת (pronounced: *beit hakneset*) in Hebrew - a "house of gathering". The word Synagogue familiar to most English speakers is a Greek equivalent of this term. In both instances, the language describes a "congress of the people" and comes from the verb לִכְנוֹס *(liknos)* which means to collect, to gather, to assemble.

Coincidently the word for Church in Hebrew is - כְּנֵסִיָּה (pronounced: *knesiya*) "a place of gathering." In a biblical context, many types of gatherings exist.

In Esther 4:16 Mordechai was told to assemble and organize all Jews of Susa to fast jointly. In Nehemiah 12:22 the priests were commanded to gather (collect) the first fruits and tithes. In Psalm 33:7 God gathers the waters and holds them together. In Ezekiel 29:38 the LORD gathers the exiles to return them to his land.

In all these examples the Hebrew words are almost identical, but the purposes of the gathering are different. A gathering usually has a clear purpose. And assembling together for worship should never be treated as all other meetings. When we gather to worship, the one whom we worship is in our midst and this type of assembly כְּנֶסֶת *(kneset)* with God is most precious.

PRAYER: *Shepherd of Israel, you have called your children to yourself from near and far. From the East and from the West, from the North and from the South, you gather us together. Those who were far off were drawn and invited to the great feast for your name's sake. You have gathered the outcasts and exiles, Oh, Redeemer. You have opened your courts to the widows and orphans, to the foreigners and aliens who fear your great name.*

You are our Savior, one who gathers us to yourself, as mother bird with outspread wings seeking to comfort and nurture. We're drawn to you, Oh, Rock of our Salvation, because deep inside we know that we belong with you. Your blessings fill our storehouses and we sing your songs at our tables. Be glorified in the fields and valleys, by the streams of water and on the well-worn paths. Be glorified in the crowded gatherings of your people and in the solitude and quietness of their souls.

DAY 39 - GEMATRIA

SCRIPTURE: *So all the generations from Abraham to David are fourteen generations; from David to the deportation to Babylon, fourteen generations; and from the deportation to Babylon to the Messiah, fourteen generations (Matt. 1:17).*

When we read the Bible, we encounter both words and numbers. It is easy and natural to focus on the meaning of words, but numbers (as in this genealogical record) can appear unimportant to us. Many people do not realize that in ancient Hebrew numbers are represented by the alphabet letters and they spell things! Imagine that A = 1 and B = 2 and C = 3 and so on, but only in Hebrew. Gematria is a Jewish interpretive method that first calculates the numerical value of a particular word, and then interprets it in different ways including matching it with another word with the same numerical sum to show a spiritual connection.

For example, in Jacob's famous dream of a stairway, the word סֻלָּם (pronounced: *sulam*) often translated as "ladder" has a numerical value of 130. Samek (ס) is 60 + Lamed (ל) is 30 + Mem (ם) is 40 = 130. Mount Sinai in Hebrew (סיני; *sinai*) adds up to the same sum so some Jewish commentaries connect Jacob's dream and Israel's reception of the ten commandments at Sinai as related events.

The record of Jesus' genealogy in Matthew uses Jewish Gematria even in Greek. To see Gematria connections one only needs to know the symbolism of numbers and how to spell those Greek words in Hebrew. Matthew highlights three spans of 14 (fourteen) generations between Abraham and David, then the same between David and Babylon, and then Babylon and Messiah (Matt.1:17). The triple repetition is the author's clue to the symbolism of the number! The value of David's name in Hebrew (דוד; *David*) is 14. Dalet (ד) is 4 + Vav (ו) is 6 + Dalet (ד) is 4 = 14. The gospel summarizes history in three sets of 14 (fourteen) generations all leading up to Messiah, saying "David, David, David".

Although Gematria, as it is now used in some Jewish circles, was certainly not implemented at the time of gospel composition, we have clear evidence that some of its principles were already in use. Matthew's theological point that he wants his readers to see in the Gematria he uses is that Yeshua (Jesus) is the "son of David" (בן דוד) the long-awaited King of Israel. He says this plainly in Matthew 1:1 and then demonstrates it through the Gematria of the genealogy that follows. When numbers are letters they begin to speak quite literally!

PRAYER: *God of Creation, Lord of Hosts, you have set the lights in the sky, you created a diversity of plants, animals, and fish. All life obeys you as you command the seas and tides and all of your creation. Even the languages of men you ordered in your doings. LORD, we are always hungry for a greater understanding of ourselves within your world. And language helps us glean the meaning that is all around us, and ever numbers speak when you imbue them with your purpose. If we could know today, Oh, Mighty God, the glimpses of the plan you have for us and our children. We probably would dance as David danced before you. Be praised, Creator, Master, LORD of All who dwells above in majesty.*

DAY 40 - CHANUKAH

SCRIPTURE: *At that time the Feast of the Dedication took place at Jerusalem; it was winter, and Jesus was walking in the temple in the portico of Solomon. The Jews then gathered around Him, and were saying to Him, "How long will You keep us in suspense? If You are the Christ, tell us plainly" (John 10:22-24).*

Solomon built the Temple in Jerusalem around 957 BCE and Babylonians destroyed it in 586 BCE. Zerubbabel restored Solomon's Temple around 515 BCE and in 167 BCE the Syrians desecrated and took over the Temple. A group of devout Jews fought back and eventually liberated the holy place from Syrians in 160 BCE. For eight days the Feast of Dedication or Chanukkah commemorates those events. In 20 BCE Herod the Great started the expansion of Zerubbabel's era buildings and completed his massive expansion in 26 CE. This rebuilding project likely involved near-complete demolition of the Zerubbabel's temple and rebuilding almost from scratch the Temple of Herod the Great.

The winter Feast of Dedication in this story is the Jewish holiday of Chanukah חֲנֻכָּה (pronounced: *Chanukah* with "ch" like a hard "h" sound). The celebration is inextricably tied to the Jerusalem Temple and miracles that occurred there long ago. It is often called a Festival of Lights because it is celebrated with the lighting of nine-light lamps. The word חֲנֻכָּה *(Chanukah)* means "dedication" and comes from verb לַחֲנוֹךְ (pronounced *lachanoch*), which means to "consecrate", to "inaugurate" and even to "enlighten", to "educate" and to "train" in some contexts. The Hebrew word for "education" is חִנּוּךְ (pronounced: *chinuch*) – "dedicated learning". The "dedication" refers to the rededication of the Jerusalem Temple back to God.

PRAYER: *Emanuel, God who is with us, come and deliver us today, reign over us as only LORD and King! Long ago your people sought to be ruled by kings rather than lean on you alone. The desire to be like other nations led them astray from you. We are no different today. You are one who sets those who rule over us and you are the one who brings them down in your time. You hold their will and their hearts in your hand, and nothing escapes your knowledge or will. We know this, yet so often we place so much faith in mere men who are but your servants. Lord God, our mighty king, if only men could know your will today with clarity. We need your judgment and your counsel. You promised restoration of all things, a glorious age, to which we look with hope. Unite us LORD in faith and trust to wait when you return to Zion!*

Printed in Great Britain
by Amazon